NORSE MYTHOLOGY

FRIGG

BY AMY C. REA

Kids Core
An Imprint of Abdo Publishing
abdobooks.com

abdobooks.com

Published by Abdo Publishing, a division of ABDO, PO Box 398166, Minneapolis, Minnesota 55439. Copyright © 2024 by Abdo Consulting Group, Inc. International copyrights reserved in all countries. No part of this book may be reproduced in any form without written permission from the publisher. Kids Core™ is a trademark and logo of Abdo Publishing.

Printed in the United States of America, North Mankato, Minnesota.
052023
092023

THIS BOOK CONTAINS RECYCLED MATERIALS

Cover Photos: Shutterstock Images (background, Frigg)
Interior Photos: German Vizulis/Shutterstock Images, 4–5; Good Studio/Shutterstock Images, 7 (birds, animals, snakes), 7 (fire); Notion Pic/Shutterstock Images, 7 (water); Sky Designs/Shutterstock Images, 7 (iron); Andrii Malysh/Shutterstock Images, 7 (stones); Kalinin Ilya/Shutterstock Images, 7 (dirt); Shutterstock Images, 7 (trees); Janis Abolins/Shutterstock Images, 7 (diseases and poisons); Liliya Butenko/Shutterstock Images, 7 (Frigg), 28 (top); Chronicle/Alamy, 8; Ivy Close Images/Alamy, 10–11, 14, 28 (bottom), 29 (bottom); Harry Collins Photography/Shutterstock Images, 13; Bettmann/Contributor/Getty Images, 17; Roberto E/Shutterstock Images, 18; Michelle Bridges/Alamy, 19; Fine Art Images/Heritage Images/Hulton Archive/Getty Images, 20, 29 (top); Jay Maidment/Marvel Studios/Photo 12/Alamy, 22–23; Yuriy Kulik/Shutterstock Images, 25; Grethe Ulgjell/Alamy, 26

Editor: Katharine Hale
Series Designer: Katharine Hale

Library of Congress Control Number: 2022949114

Publisher's Cataloging-in-Publication Data

Names: Rea, Amy C., author.
Title: Frigg / by Amy C. Rea
Description: Minneapolis, Minnesota: Abdo Publishing Company, 2024 | Series: Norse mythology | Includes online resources and index.
Identifiers: ISBN 9781098291198 (lib. bdg.) | ISBN 9781098277376 (ebook)
Subjects: LCSH: Mythology, Norse--Juvenile literature. | Frigg (Norse deity)--Juvenile literature. | Gods--Juvenile literature. | Divinities--Juvenile literature.
Classification: DDC 293.13--dc23

CONTENTS

CHAPTER 1
Baldr's Dreams 4

CHAPTER 2
The Goddess Frigg 10

CHAPTER 3
Frigg's Importance 22

Legendary Facts 28
Glossary 30
Online Resources 31
Learn More 31
Index 32
About the Author 32

Baldr is a Norse god representing courage, wisdom, and light.

BALDR'S DREAMS

Baldr startles awake, shaking in fear. He just had a terrible dream where he died. He has had this dream before, and it scares him. Baldr's parents are Odin and Frigg. They are the leaders of the gods. Baldr decides to ask them for help.

The gods meet to decide how to protect Baldr. The dreams do not say how he will die. Frigg decides she must take action. She goes on a long journey. She makes every creature and thing promise they will not hurt Baldr. When she returns home, she is exhausted. She hopes her plan will work. But she worries that this dream will come true. It scares her. All she can do is wait and see.

Frigg and Odin

Frigg's husband, Odin, is a powerful and smart god. Frigg is also smart. She often makes bets with him and wins. Norse myths show her as Odin's equal. She is known as the queen of the gods.

Protecting Baldr

- Fire
- Water
- Stones
- Iron and other metals
- Diseases and poisons
- Trees
- Birds
- Animals
- Dirt
- Snakes

Frigg traveled throughout the world to make all things promise not to hurt Baldr.

One of Frigg's powers is seeing the future.

Norse Mythology

Frigg is one of the most important goddesses in Norse mythology. Norse mythology is made up of stories from the religion of early northern Germanic peoples. Most surviving Norse myths come from **Scandinavia**. These stories tell about the lives and actions of gods, goddesses, giants, wolves, dragons, elves, dwarfs, and regular people.

The Norse people believed the world began when the gods killed a giant and used his body to create the world. Nine main areas made up this world. These were called the nine worlds. The Norse people believed their world would be destroyed at an event called Ragnarok. They believed that Frigg was one of the few gods and goddesses who would survive Ragnarok.

Further Evidence

Look at the website below. Does it give any new evidence to support Chapter One?

Frigg

abdocorelibrary.com/frigg

Frigg's husband is Odin, the leader of the gods.

CHAPTER 2

THE GODDESS FRIGG

Frigg has fewer surviving myths than some of the other Norse gods and goddesses. There is not much information about her family. One Norse myth says Frigg's father is Fjorgynn. Frigg is married to Odin. Baldr is their son. Odin has many other sons.

Hodr is one of them. Stories are not clear on whether Frigg has other children.

Frigg is the goddess of **fertility**, love, and marriage. She has a **garment** made of falcon or hawk feathers. In one myth, the **trickster** god

Frigg and Freya

Frigg has many similarities with the goddess Freya. Both are goddesses of fertility. They both own magical feathered garments. Many scholars think they might have once been the same goddess. They think as stories changed over time, this goddess became both Frigg and Freya. There were important differences between the goddesses. Frigg lived in a place called Fensalir, while Freya lived in Folkvangar. Frigg was a member of the group of gods called the Aesir. Freya was a member of the Vanir.

The gods can use Frigg's magic feathers to transform into a bird.

Loki uses Frigg's feathered garment and turns into a bird. He is captured by the giant Geirrod. In exchange for his freedom, Loki promises to bring the god Thor so Geirrod can fight him.

Gna and Fulla are two of the goddesses who serve Frigg.

Frigg and Other Goddesses

Many of the other goddesses serve Frigg. An *eski* is a wooden box made from ash trees. It is usually used to carry personal items. The goddess Fulla carries Frigg's *eski* for her. Fulla also takes care of Frigg's shoes and shares secrets with her. Lofn has permission from Frigg and Odin to arrange marriages. Hlin guards people whom Frigg wants to protect. Gna is a goddess with a horse that can fly and swim. Frigg sends Gna on errands to other lands.

Odin and Frigg

Myths about Frigg often show her tricking her husband. One of these stories involves a war. The Winnili were from Scandinavia.

The Vandals were a larger Germanic group. The two groups were about to fight each other in a war. Both peoples asked Odin for victory. Odin supported the Vandals. But Frigg supported the Winnili. Odin told Frigg whomever he saw first on the day of the battle would be the winners. Odin was sure he would see the Vandals first.

Frigg told the Winnili women to style their long hair to look like beards. She told them to stand with their men on the battlefield. Then she turned Odin's bed so he would see them first. When Odin woke up, he asked, "Who are these Longbeards?" Frigg said because he had named them, he should give them the victory. The Longbeards were eventually called the Lombards.

The Lombards were a real people who moved south from Scandinavia into the rest of Europe. They controlled land in modern-day Italy until the 700s CE.

Mistletoe grows on other plants, stealing their resources.

Baldr's Death

All of the gods knew of Frigg's journey to protect Baldr. They made a game of throwing things at him. Since Baldr could not be killed, everything bounced off of him. But Loki made a discovery. Frigg had not made the mistletoe plant swear the oath. She thought the plant was too young to make the promise.

Loki disguised himself as an old woman to ask Frigg whether anything had not sworn the oath to protect Baldr.

Loki left to find the mistletoe plant. Then he went back to where the gods were playing with Baldr. The blind god Hodr was standing away from the others. Hodr was Baldr's brother.

Baldr's death was a great tragedy for the gods.

Loki asked why Hodr was not playing with the other gods. Hodr said it was because he was blind and had no weapon. Loki helped Hodr aim the mistletoe. Hodr threw it as hard as he could. It struck Baldr in the chest. Baldr died immediately. All of Frigg's efforts were useless. She was heartbroken at the loss of her son.

PRIMARY SOURCE

In the poem *Lokasenna*, or "Loki's Taunts," Loki insults the other gods. After he insults Frigg, Freya responds:

> I believe that Frigg
>
> Knows everyone's fate,
>
> Even if she never speaks of it.

Source: Jackson Crawford, translator. *The Poetic Edda: Stories of the Norse Gods and Heroes.* Hackett, 2015, p. 106.

Comparing Texts

Think about the quote. Does it support the information in this chapter? Or does it give a different perspective? Explain how in a few sentences.

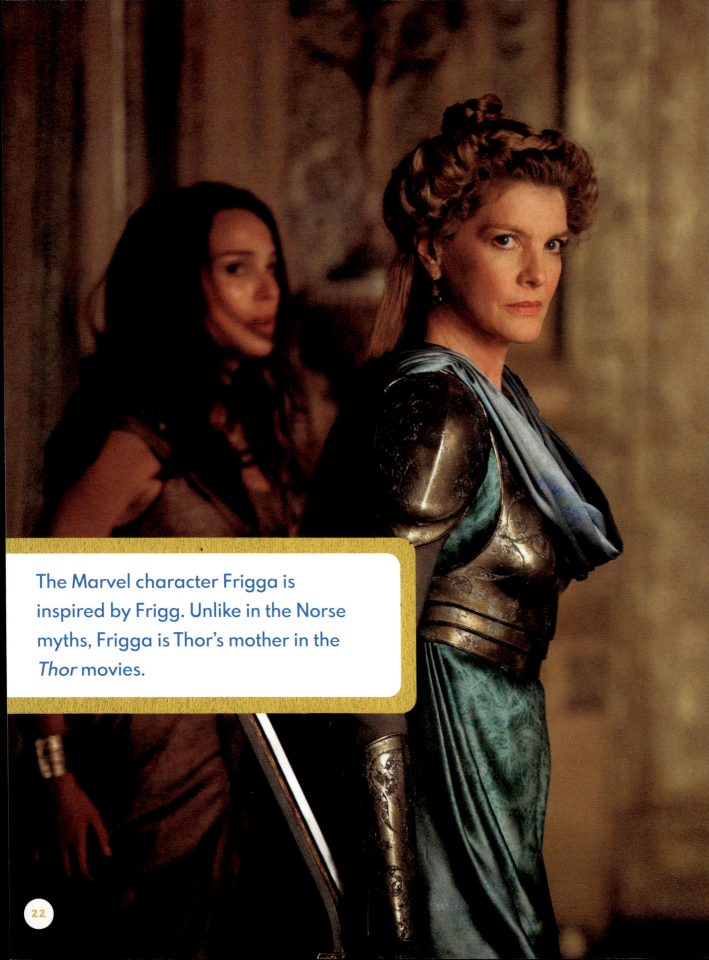

The Marvel character Frigga is inspired by Frigg. Unlike in the Norse myths, Frigga is Thor's mother in the *Thor* movies.

CHAPTER 3

FRIGG'S IMPORTANCE

Frigg had many important roles in Norse mythology. She was a goddess of fertility, marriage, family, and motherhood. Her son was extremely important to her, and she was fiercely protective of him. She could see into the future, and she was very smart.

Frigg is one of the few gods who will survive the end of the world at Ragnarok. But her husband Odin will be killed. Old Norse and **Viking** women often lost sons and husbands to disease, battles, and shipwrecks. Having already lost Baldr, Frigg would become both a grieving mother and **widow**. Many Norse women would have understood Frigg's grief.

Frigg in Art

There is little surviving art of Frigg created by the Norse people. But a cathedral in Schleswig, Germany, has artwork from the High to Late Middle Ages (1000–1500 CE). There are paintings of two women. One is riding a cat, and one is riding a **distaff**. Some scholars think

The constellation known today as Orion's Belt was called Frigg's Distaff by the Norse people.

these women might be Freya and Frigg. Over the centuries, many artists have illustrated Frigg. Artists often show her on a throne with the goddesses who serve her. This is a sign of Frigg's importance. Other artists show Frigg with babies. In many works of art, Frigg is holding a distaff. In Norse stories, **seers** could use a distaff to help predict the future. Norse mythology says Frigg could see the future.

A wood carving honoring Frigg is on display at the city hall in Oslo, Norway.

Frigg was an important goddess to the Norse people. She is known as a devoted mother and Odin's equal. She is a powerful goddess who remains popular today.

Frigg and Friday

Many days of the week are named after Norse gods. *Friday* likely comes from *Frigg's Day*. Some scholars think it could also come from *Freya's Day*.

Joshua J. Mark writes about ancient history. In an article about Frigg, he wrote:

> In all her stories, Frigg is a completely independent woman—even seeming to live apart from her husband in her own land with her own palace—and her popularity no doubt [came], at least in part, from this aspect of her personality.

Source: Joshua J. Mark, "Frigg," *World History Encyclopedia*, 27 Aug. 2021, worldhistory.org. Accessed 7 Oct. 2022.

What's the Big Idea?

Read this quote carefully. What is its main idea? Explain how the main idea is supported by details.

LEGENDARY FACTS

Frigg was one of the most important Norse goddesses.

Frigg could see into the future. Her husband was Odin.

Frigg tried to prevent her son Baldr from dying but was unsuccessful.

Many goddesses served Frigg.

Glossary

distaff
a tool that holds material to be spun into thread or yarn

fertility
the ability to create life and support growth

garment
a piece of clothing

Scandinavia
the countries of Norway, Sweden, and Denmark, and sometimes Iceland and Finland

seers
people who are said to have the power to see the future

trickster
a person who plays pranks or tricks on someone else

Viking
referring to warriors and sailors from Scandinavia who lived from the 800s to the mid-1000s CE

widow
a wife whose spouse has died

Online Resources

To learn more about Frigg, visit our free resource websites below.

Visit **abdocorelibrary.com** or scan this QR code for free Common Core resources for teachers and students, including vetted activities, multimedia, and booklinks, for deeper subject comprehension.

Visit **abdobooklinks.com** or scan this QR code for free additional online weblinks for further learning. These links are routinely monitored and updated to provide the most current information available.

Learn More

Conley, Kate. *Odin*. Abdo, 2024.

Ralphs, Matt. *Norse Myths*. DK Children, 2021.

Steele, Philip. *Vikings*. DK Children, 2018.

Index

art, 24–25

Baldr, 5–6, 7, 11, 18–20, 23–24

distaffs, 24–25

feathers, 12–13
fertility, 12, 23
Freya, 12, 21, 25, 26

Germany, 24

Hodr, 12, 19–20

Loki, 12–13, 18–20
Lombards, 15–16

mistletoe, 18–20

Odin, 5, 6, 11, 15–16, 24, 26

Ragnarok, 9, 24

Scandinavia, 8, 15

Vikings, 24

About the Author

Amy C. Rea is the author of several children's books. She also writes about travel and food in Minnesota. She lives in Saint Anthony, Minnesota, with her husband and silly dog.